Swedish Christmas A-Z (Plus 3!)

An Alphabet Coloring & Activity Book

This Keepsake Book Belongs To:

_____

Swedish Christmas A-Z (Plus 3!)
An Alphabet Coloring & Activity Book

What does A-Z (Plus 3!) mean?

The Swedish alphabet has the same 26 letters as the English alphabet, A-Z, PLUS three additional letters. They are: Å, Ä, Ö. That's 29 letters in all! BUT some of the Swedish people would say they have 28 letters, because they do not really count the letter W (which is used only in names and pronounced as a V). That has been changing as the Swedish alphabet more actively includes the letter W, especially because of the world-wide web!

What am I going to do in this book? You will ...

- Explore Swedish Christmas traditions with the alphabet as your guide.
- Learn to pronounce the Swedish word for the letter. Some of the words look like the English words but most are pronounced differently.
- Read about the tradition.
- Color the heading and illustration on each page. This will make it your own special book.
- Do the activities and answer the questions with your family or friends.
- Look for tomte/jultomte throughout this book. Not tomten or jultomten (the difference will be explained on Page 61). Count this one too! May not look exactly like this tomte but each has a beard and a hat. How many do you find? Answer is on Page 88.
- Use the blank pages to add your own personal touch through stories, memories, photos, drawings, and recipes. Enjoy!

Very important: What else do I need to know before I begin?

- Use caution when working with cooking and craft tools and supplies.
- Use extreme caution when using candles and flames. Never leave a lit candle unattended.
- Close adult supervision is important at all times. We want you to have fun and be safe!

Swedish Christmas A-Z (Plus 3!): An Alphabet Coloring & Activity Book
Copyright © 2007-2023 by Kathy Bernstrom Lerfald
ISBN: 978-0-9801187-0-4
Available from Amazon.com and other retail outlets
Published by S&C Resources. All rights reserved. No part of this book may be reproduced, stored in a retrieval system, or transmitted in any form or by any means – electronic, mechanical, photocopy, recording, scanning or otherwise – except for brief quotations for critical review or articles, without the prior written permission of the copyright holder.
Facebook: www.facebook.com/swedishtraditionsandholidays/ (this is an open group)
Facebook: www.facebook.com/groups/swedishcultureandtraditionsforkids/ (this is by request)
Tack så mycket (Thanks very much) to Greta & Jonas Lann, Ewa Rydåker, and Gunvor Karlsson.

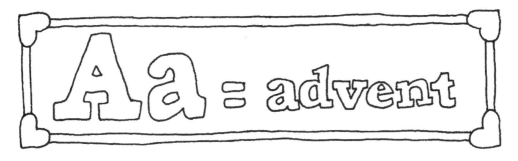

Pronounced: ahd-VENT

The Swedish Christmas season begins on "Advent Sunday," four Sundays before Christmas Day. This time leading up to Christmas is called Advent, which means arrival or coming. Candles are lit, one each Sunday until Christmas Day.

- Pronounce the Swedish word. Color the heading and picture above.
- Gather four candles and group them together in candleholders to create your own Advent countdown display. (Use candles with adult supervision.)
- Light the first candle four Sundays before Christmas Day. Allow it to burn about one-fourth down. Light an additional candle each Sunday, burning about one-fourth of each candle lit. By the fourth Sunday all four will be lit.

5

6

Pronounced: byell-er-klung

Jingle bells (bjällerklang) ring throughout Sweden during the Christmas season. They are heard from the horse-driven sleighs. They are heard in homes, used as ornaments on the Christmas tree or above the doorways. It's one of the joyful, happy Christmas sounds.

Jingle!
Jingle!
Cling!
Cling!
Clang!
Clang!

- This is a long word but has a fun sound to it. Learn to pronounce bjällerklang. Color the heading and picture above.
- Find a bell in your home – any kind of bell. Ring it at a certain time each day during the Christmas season. Would ringing it just before dinner be a good time for you and your family? Listen to the <u>sound</u> of your bell.

Pronounced: shoo-CLAAD

No Christmas season would be complete without chocolates. And it's a must for the Christmas table of treats. Aladdin® is the box of chocolates that every family in Sweden buys at Christmas. Oftentimes choklad (which means chocolate or chocolates) also contain almonds and raisins. It's a sweet tradition!

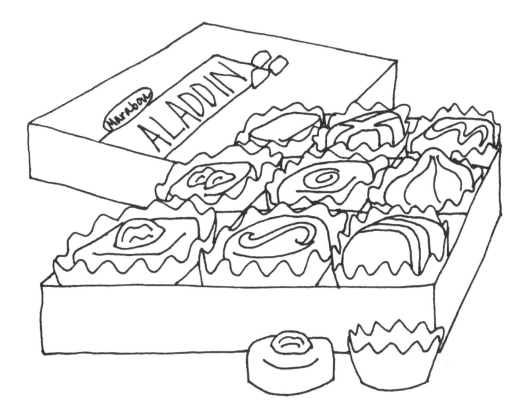

- Pronounce the Swedish word. Color the heading and picture above.
- Do you eat chocolates at Christmas? If you do, what is your favorite kind of chocolates? What Christmas candy sweets are traditions for you and your family? See Page 11 for a simple chocolate candy recipe.

Ischoklad Candy Recipe

CAUTION: Must be with adult supervision!

Ischoklad (ice chocolate)

There are many recipes for ischoklad.
Here's an easy one:
1 cup semi-sweet chocolate chips
1/2 cup virgin coconut oil
(unrefined)
(the formula is twice as much
chocolate as coconut oil)
Small foil candy cups*

Combine chocolate chips and coconut
oil in a metal bowl over a boiling pan of
water until it's melted. Carefully pour
mixture into cups and refrigerate.
Keep refrigerated and serve cold.

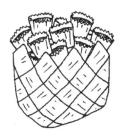

*These can be difficult to find. You could use a baking pan (perhaps 9" x 9") lined
with parchment paper. "Or, we poured the melted mixture onto a cookie sheet lined
with parchment paper and clipped the four ends with clothespins to contain the
mixture! (Sometimes you just have to be inventive!) We broke it into pieces and
served it that way. Important to serve right from the refrigerator so it maintains the
'cold' taste." KBL

My favorite Christmas candies are ...

Dd = dekoration

Pronounced: de-corah-SHUNE

The Christmas tree is brought into the Swedish home a day or two before Christmas Eve. It needs to be decorated! A dekoration (decoration) of a woven paper heart (julgranskorg) is popular. So is the decoration of a Christmas "cracker" (julgranskaramel) filled with candy.

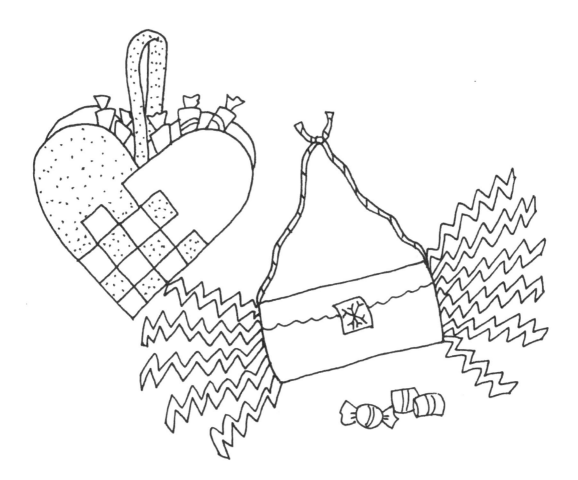

- Pronounce the Swedish word. Color the heading and picture above.
- Make one or both of the special decorations that the Swedish children (and adults) love to use on their Christmas trees. Why not put them on your Christmas tree this year? Directions for both the julgranskorg and the julgranskaramel are on the following pages.

13

Julgranskorg

1. Fold a piece of paper in half and trace the pattern at the right.

2. In another color (blue & yellow are traditional Swedish colors), cut an identical "twin" piece. You could use the first pattern to cut the second pattern.

3. Cut three identical slits in each piece.

4. Weave the two together (and this can be tricky).

5. For strips 1 and 3, go through a row on the other twin and then surround the next row … through a row, surround a row.

6. For strips 2 and 4, start by surround a row, then through a row, surround a row and through a row. In this way you will be able to open the heart and it can be a basket.

7. And if it didn't work, just weave the rows over and under the other twin's rows and glue down the ends of the rows. You won't be able to open it, but it will still look cute on your tree.

8. Cut a strip of paper for the handle (out of either color) and glue it to the basket.

9. Hang it on your Christmas tree!

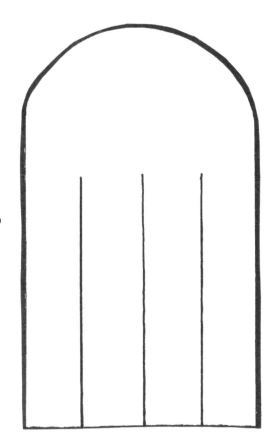

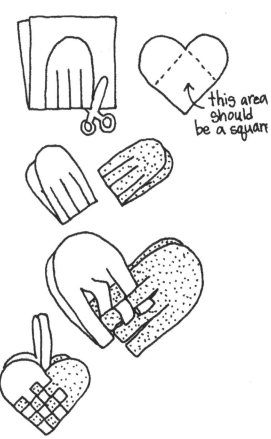

this area should be a square

Julgranskaramel

1. Cut a 4″x 4″ piece of cardstock.

2. Roll it into a cylinder so it's about one inch in diameter. Secure it with tape.

3. Lay the roll in the middle of a stack of three pieces of tissue paper (three different colors).

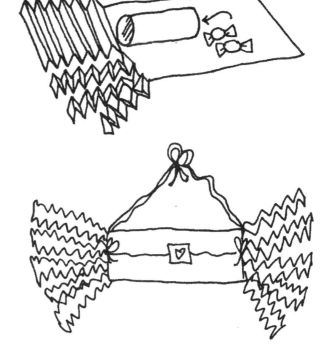

4. Mark how wide the tube is and then fold the tissue like an accordion until you reach the tube.

5. Cut the tissue into 1/2 inch wide strips.

6. Put your favorite individually-wrapped candies inside the tube.

7. Wrap the tissue around the tube and secure it with tape or a holiday sticker.

8. Tie a ribbon on each end of the tube (around the tissue) to close the ends AND secure a ribbon to the tube to be able to hang it on your tree.

9. Fluff out the tissue and hang it on your tree. Eat the candy after Christmas!

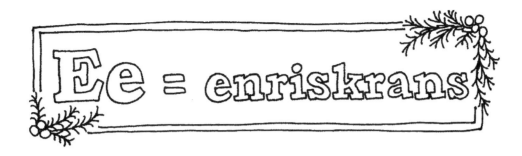

Ee = enriskrans

Pronounced: en-reese-krans

Enriskrans is a juniper twig wreath. Most of the people of Sweden hang a wreath outside of their doors at Christmastime. Some are made of lingonberry twigs or moss, and many are made out of juniper twigs. It is a welcoming sight!

- Pronounce the Swedish word. Color the heading and picture above.
- Do you have a wreath on your door at Christmastime? If you do, what is your wreath made out of? How is it decorated? Draw a wreath on Page 21.

My wreath ...

My wreath ...

Pronounced: frookt

Frukt (fruit) is an important part of Christmas in Sweden, especially oranges. Bowls of them sit around homes and fill the rooms with a delightful citrus scent. Why not pick one up and eat it as you wait for your meal? Or you might see a bowl of oranges with whole cloves poked into them in an interesting design.

- Pronounce the Swedish word. Color the heading and picture above.
- Gather some oranges and have them available for eating. You could also poke whole cloves into a few and display them in a bowl. Notice the wonderful aroma.

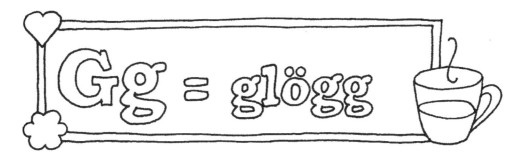

Pronounced: glugg

Glögg is a very popular Swedish Christmas drink throughout the season. It is a warm, mulled wine with raisins and almonds. There are even glögg parties! Often glögg is served with ginger cookies (see letter P).

Children's Fruit Juice Glögg

1 orange (zest & rind)
4 cups apple cider
2 cups white grape juice
3 tablespoons sugar
1 cinnamon stick (about 3-4 inches)
8-10 whole cloves (to taste)
1/2 cup raisins
1/2 cup blanched (whole) almonds

1. Wash the orange and peel the zest & rind from it.
2. Combine the orange zest & rind, cider, white grape juice, sugar, cinnamon stick and cloves in a kettle. Stir and cover.
3. Let it stand for 2 hours.
4. Heat the mixture to boiling over medium high heat.
5. Reduce the heat to low and simmer for 30 minutes (covered).
6. Strain out any remaining spices and peels.
7. Serve warm with a few raisins and almonds in each serving cup.
Simple version: Heat apple cider with a cinnamon stick. Add the raisins and almonds to each cup.

- Pronounce the Swedish word. Color the heading and picture above.
- Make this special fruit version of the glögg drink using the recipe above.
- Use the following toast when you drink your glögg together: "God Jul" (good-yule) which means Merry Christmas.

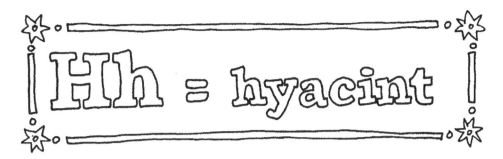

Hh = hyacint

Pronounced: hee-a-CINT

The hyacint (hyacinth in English) is the most popular indoor flower in Sweden at Christmas. They come in many different varieties, and their fragrance fills the homes with sweetness. Other popular flowers include the poinsettia, tulip and the amaryllis.

- Pronounce the Swedish word. Color the heading and the picture above. Most Christmas hyacinths in Sweden are blue, pink or white in color. What color or colors do you want your hyacinths to be in your picture?
- If you want to force a hyacinth bulb to bloom, do this: Put a bulb or bulbs in a paper bag in your refrigerator for about 4-6 weeks. When you take them out, put each in its own specially designed forcing vase (available in stores). Fill the vase with water, just below the bottom of the bulb. If water touches the bottom of the bulb it will rot. Place the vase in a bright window and you will have a beautiful, scented hyacinth flower in about 4 weeks. Unless you started it a few weeks before Christmas, it will not be blooming for Christmas but will brighten your wintertime whenever it blooms.

 Hej! (pronounced hay) – means Hi! in Swedish

Pronounced: ease-lickta

Lights! Lights! Everywhere! Indoor lights. Outdoor lights. It's important to light up the dark Swedish Christmas season. One of those ways is to make an islykta (ice lantern). It sparkles! It glistens! It celebrates Christmas and winter.

1. Fill an orange juice or milk carton about 2/3 full with water.
2. Place the container in the freezer for several hours (if it's a 1/2 gallon size it will take an estimated 3-6 hours or more). It's ready when the top and sides of the container have layers of ice on them, but you can see that there's still water inside.
3. Take the container out of the freezer and flip it upside down. Remove the ice chunk from the container (you may need to use some warm water).
4. There will be a very thin layer of ice on the flipped end. Gently break through that layer of ice and pour out the water.
5. Place a votive candle in the "hole" and carefully light it.

NOTE: Your islykta will look more like the one in the header than in the picture above.

- Pronounce the Swedish word. Color the heading and picture above.
- Make an islykta using the instructions above. Put it outside and let it glisten during the winter evenings. If you can't put it outside because it will melt, put it on a plate or in a large bowl and use it as a centerpiece for one of your Christmas season meals.

Pronounced: yule

Jul means Christmas. The letter J is pronounced as a Y in Swedish. God Jul (good yule) is Merry Christmas! There are many words that begin with jul: Julafton (Christmas Eve), Juldagen (Christmas Day), Julbord (a family Christmas Eve meal), julklappar (Christmas presents), julkärve (a special sheaf of wheat for the birds, outside on a pole) are just a few. Jul is a good word to know!

- Pronounce the Swedish word. Color the heading and picture above.
- On Page 35, you will find more words with Jul! Do you want to make Swedish meatballs for one of your Christmas meals?
- Then on Page 37, there's a picture of the Julbord. Julbord is like a Swedish smörgåsbord (a buffet with a variety of food choices) but with special Christmas foods.

Swedish Meatballs

If you live near an IKEA® or a Scandinavian deli, you could probably purchase Swedish meatballs (or the meat mixture to form and fry/bake them). If you wish to make them yourself, here's a simple recipe:

1 pound lean ground beef
1/2 cup dried breadcrumbs (fine)
1 egg
1/2 cup milk (2% or whole)
flour
(sauce is optional: see below)

1/4 cup finely chopped onion or
1 tablespoon minced onion
1/2 teaspoon salt (or more/to taste)
1/8 teaspoon pepper
1/4 teaspoon nutmeg

Combine all ingredients and form into small meatballs, less than one inch in diameter. Roll formed meatballs in flour and place in frying pan with cooking oil. Brown the meatballs. Now you've got a choice: After the meatballs are browned thoroughly, add water, cover the frying pan and simmer 20-25 minutes OR pour off the fat and place the meatballs in a casserole and add the following sauce: Mix together 1 can cream of mushroom soup, 1/2 cup milk and 1/2 cup sour cream and pour over meatballs. Bake at 350 degrees Fahrenheit for one hour, covered.

Kk = Knutdagen

Pronounced: knoot-doggen (k is not silent)

The Swedish Christmas season begins on Advent Sunday and ends on Knutdagen (the Knut Day) which is January 13. Knutdagen is more commonly known as Tjugondag Knut (Twentieth Day Knut) or hilarymas. On Knutdagen the family strips the Christmas tree of all of its decorations, eats the candy inside of "crackers" on the tree and throws it out! There is dancing and singing, and the last Christmas meal is eaten. Now less than 11 months before Christmas starts all over again!

- Pronounce the Swedish word. Color the heading and picture above.
- Did you know that in Sweden there are "name days"? So in addition to your birthday, there will be a specific day each year that celebrates everyone with a certain name! For example, the "name day" for everyone with the name John is May 3. January 13 is the Knut day, named for King Knut in Scandinavian history. If you could choose a "name day" for yourself, what date would you pick? _____

Pronounced: yuse

Ljus (light) is so important during the dark Swedish Christmas season. There are Advent candles, Lucia lights, ice lanterns, and in the Swedish homes there are also lights hanging in the windows, lighted wooden candelabras sitting on window ledges, and strings of lights.

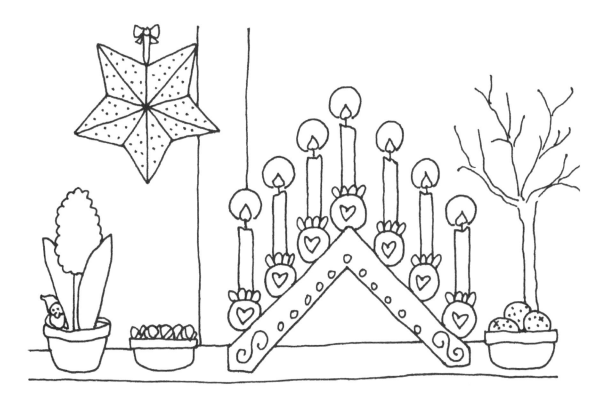

- Pronounce the Swedish word. Color the heading and picture above.
- Do you live in a part of the world that has shorter-lighted days at Christmastime? If you do, what lights do you use? If you live where there are longer-lighted days, how do you use and celebrate light at Christmas?

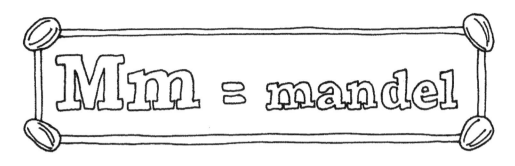

Pronounced: mun-dell

Mandel is an almond. One of the Swedish traditions that's especially fun is that of hiding an almond in a bowl of rice porridge (gröt) or rice pudding. As the individual portions are spooned into bowls, no one knows who will get the almond. And the one who does will be the next one to get married! That's the traditional meaning. Or the one who gets the almond gets an additional gift! Choose a meaning you like.

Rice Pudding

1 & 1/2 cups cooked white rice
1/3 to 1/2 cup sugar (to taste)
2 cups milk (2% or whole)
3 eggs (beaten)
1/2 teaspoon salt
1 teaspoon vanilla
1/2 cup raisins (optional)
ground cinnamon (optional)
1 whole blanched almond

Combine all ingredients (except cinnamon & almond) and pour it into a baking dish. Bake at 350 degrees Fahrenheit for 25 minutes. Stir, add almond, sprinkle cinnamon on top.
Bake for an additional 20-25 minutes (or until set).

CAUTION: Watch for the almond when eating!

- Pronounce the Swedish word. Color the heading and picture above.
- Add an almond to one of your favorite Christmas recipes or try the rice pudding recipe above. Who do you think will find the special almond?

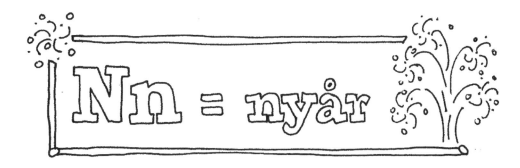

Pronounced: nyee-ore

Tucked in the long Christmas season is, of course, nyår which is the name of the holidays of New Year's Eve and New Year's Day in Sweden. At midnight on New Year's Eve all of the church bells of Stockholm ring out and there are fireworks of celebration.

- Pronounce the Swedish word. Color the heading and picture above.
- How do you celebrate New Year's Eve? New Year's Day?

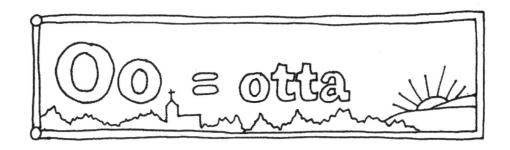

Pronounced: oh-ta

Otta means very early in the morning. On Christmas morning, before the dawn, there is a special church service called Julotta (yule oh-ta). In Sweden, many people attend this traditional service – in city cathedrals – or in quaint country churches. It's a cherished tradition.

- Pronounce the Swedish word. Color the heading and picture above.
- Is a church service part of your Christmas celebration? If it is, when is it for you? Christmas Eve? Christmas Day? Early? Late?

47

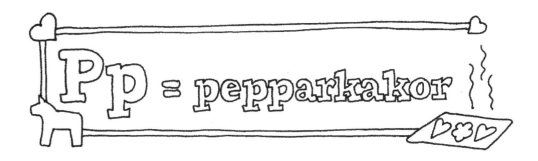

Pronounced: pepper-ka-kore

The word pepparkakor means ginger cookies. They are a popular and yummy smelling Swedish Christmas tradition. Pepparkakor are served at glögg parties, on Lucia Day and throughout the Christmas season. Gingerbread houses are also very popular.

- Pronounce the Swedish word. Color the heading and picture above. Color the gingerbread house on the next page too.
- See Page 59 for an easy ginger cookie recipe (without rolling out the dough). Or you can buy the famous brand Anna's® cookies, available at IKEA®, online and some grocery stores.
- What are your favorite cookies at Christmas? Do you buy them or make them?

pepparkakshus

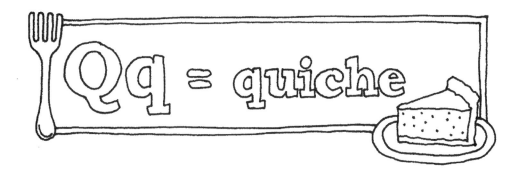

Pronounced: keesh

There are very few words in the Swedish language that begin with the letter Q. But quiche (an egg dish with various ingredients) is one of them. It is spelled, pronounced and means the same as the English word. With all the yummy ham and cheese that is served at the Christmas Eve meal, a perfect after-Christmas breakfast could be quiche.

- Pronounce the Swedish word. Color the heading and picture above.
- What is your favorite egg dish? _____
  Why not make it today or tomorrow – for breakfast or for lunch or for dinner?

Pronounced: rim

With each Christmas present, the giver has written a rim (rhyme) or a riddle hinting at what is in the gift without actually telling what it is. On December 23 when the Swedish people are doing their last-minute preparations, some are writing rhymes for their packages. There's even a television program to help people in the writing of their rhymes.

- Pronounce the Swedish word. Color the heading and picture above.
- Choose one gift that you are going to give to someone this Christmas. Write a rhyme to place on the outside of it – hint at what's in it – but don't tell! Is this easy for you to do? Could you use some help?

Pronounced: saang-ta lou-SEE-ah

Sankta Lucia (Santa Lucia/Saint Lucia/St. Lucy) was an Italian saint who has been popularized by the Swedish people. She represents light and hope. The tradition is that each December 13, the oldest daughter (this can be adjusted, of course) of the family leads the early morning procession, bringing treats and singing the Sankta Lucia song.

- Pronounce the Swedish word. Color the heading and picture above.
- Watch a YouTube presentation of Sankta Lucia. Here are three that are currently available: Christmas – Santa Lucia Sweden OR Swedish Saint Lucia posted by Carl Andersson (shows a horse and sleigh) OR Swedish Lucia for Dummies (humorous).
- See Page 59 for instructions on celebrating your own Sankta Lucia Day.

Sankta Lucia Day, December 13

Here's a simple version of having your own Sankta Lucia morning. In the early morning of December 13, have a Lucia procession, serve some treats to eat, and sing a Lucia song. It will be lots of fun!

Choose someone in your family to be Sankta Lucia (traditionally it's the oldest daughter). She wears a white dress or robe and ties a red sash around her waist. You can purchase a crown with battery-powered lights from any Scandinavian store or an on-line retailer. Do not use real candles in a crown or on the head. If you can't find something to wear in her hair, she can carry some kind of light. The name Lucia comes from the Latin word for "light." Other children in the family can be attendants with battery-operated lights or star boys with a star attached to a stick (see the book cover).

An adult needs to help in preparing the goodies to eat. Sankta Lucia usually serves coffee, lussekatter (Lucia "cats" or buns) and pepparkakor (ginger cookies). You can choose what you'd like to serve. Many pepparkakor recipes require the dough to be rolled out and cut using cookie cutters. Here's a simpler recipe that doesn't require the rolling-out part.

Pepparkakor

1 cup brown sugar	2 teaspoons baking soda
3/4 cup butter (softened)	1/2 teaspoon salt
4 teaspoons molasses	1 teaspoon ground ginger
1 egg	1 teaspoon ground cinnamon
2-1/4 cups flour	1/2 teaspoon ground cloves

Mix the butter and sugar until it is creamy. Add the egg and molasses and beat well. Mix together the dry ingredients in a separate bowl, making sure it is well mixed. Add the dry ingredients and mix again. Form the dough into small balls. Roll each ball of dough in sugar and flatten it with the bottom of a drinking glass. Bake at 350 degrees Fahrenheit for about 8-10 minutes. Cool the cookies slightly on the pan before removing them. Soft when warm and crisper as they cool.

Here are the words to a simple Sankta Lucia song (use a tune you are familiar with or make one up using these words):

Behold, in our doorway stands
Dressed in white with candles in her hair,
Sankta Lucia, Sankta Lucia

For a complete explanation of the Sankta Lucia celebration, check out Lucia Morning in Sweden by Ewa Rydåker, with illustrations by Caterina Såhlberg. A charming story of the Svensson (Swedish) family and the preparations for their Lucia celebration. Includes patterns, recipes, songs. Available from Amazon.com and other retail outlets. "Thank you to Ewa Rydåker for your encouragement and for helping with the pronunciations for this book!" KBL

Pronounced: tohm-ten

Tomten or Jultomten is the Swedish Santa Claus. Santa arrives at the door on Christmas Eve and asks, "Are there any good children here?" If there are (and there always are), he distributes gifts from his bag. If Santa has time, he may even join the family in a dance around the Christmas tree.

- Pronounce the Swedish word. Color the heading and picture above.
- A difference: Tomten is Santa Claus and tomte (singular) and tomtar (plural) are little dwarf helpers who lived in the sheds and barns of Swedish barns a long time ago (a Swedish legend).
- Does Santa come to your house? If he does, when? Christmas Eve? During the night? On Christmas morning?

61

Pronounced: upp-e-seatar-kvell

The big Christmas celebration in Sweden is December 24 (and December 25 is a quieter day). In preparation for Christmas Eve there is uppesittarkväll which is December 23. This is when the last-minute preparations are done: The knack (toffee candy) is made, the ham is tested with a piece of bread and some mustard, the last of the gifts are wrapped, the sealing wax is added, and the rhymes are written. It is a cozy evening before the big day of celebration.

sealing wax

- Pronounce the Swedish word. Color the heading and picture above.
- What are the last-minute preparations that you and your family do?

_____

_____

_____

63

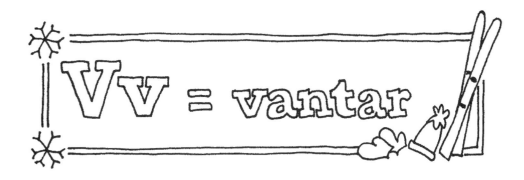

Pronounced: VAHN-tahr

If you live in a cold climate at Christmas like Sweden, mittens (vantar) are important. There is even a special type of mittens that is very popular as Christmas gifts. They are called Lovikka vantar (mittens), first made by a woman in northern Sweden in 1892. They are named after the village of Lovikka, located in the Torne Valley, Sweden.

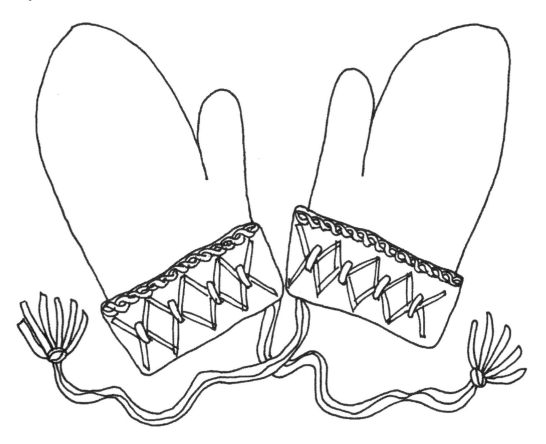

- Pronounce the Swedish word. Color the heading and picture above.
- Do you live in a cold climate where you need to wear mittens at Christmastime? Draw a pair of mittens on Page 67 that you might like to wear.

My mittens ...

Pronounced: Vil-ma & Vil-yum

The Swedish language does not generally use the letter W except for some names. Even when it is used in a name, the W is pronounced with a V sound. Wilma and William are popular children's names in Sweden. What do you think Wilma and William are doing on Christmas Eve?

- Pronounce the Swedish words. Color the heading and picture above.
- Does your name start with a W? Do you know someone who has a name that starts with a W? _____ Try saying the name with a V sound instead of a W sound.

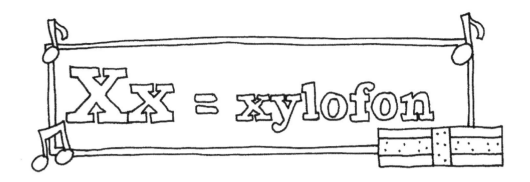

Pronounced: sule-oh-phone

Music is a big part of the Christmas season in Sweden, from the beautiful choirs singing the sacred songs of the season to the songs the families sing while dancing around the Christmas tree. AND, maybe, just maybe, a child might receive the gift of a xylofon (xylophone) from Santa. More music!

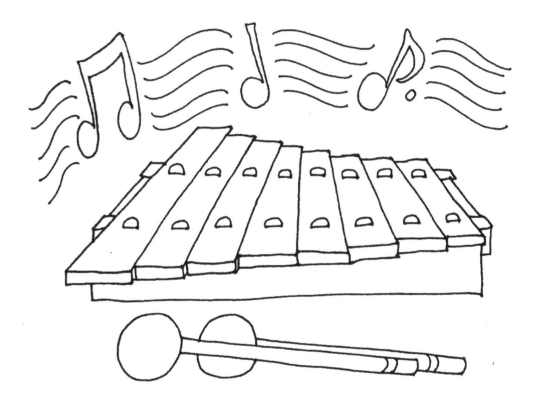

- Pronounce the Swedish word. Color the heading and picture above.
- Do you have a xylophone? If you do, try to plunk out a Christmas tune.
- Make up a tune (and sing it together) using these words from a popular Swedish song:

    "Now it is Christmas again, and now it is Christmas again,
    and Christmas lasts all the way 'till Easter."

71

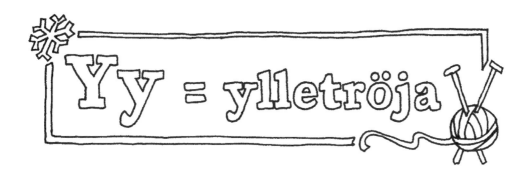

Pronounced: ull-e-tray-ah

December is cold in Sweden. It's a good idea to wear "a sweater made of wool" (ylletröja). Slippers made of soft lamb's wool are also very popular at Christmastime. Warm and cozy! Both sweaters and slippers make great gifts to give or to receive.

- Pronounce the Swedish word. Color the heading and picture above.
- Do you have a favorite sweater? Do you have a Christmas sweater? What would you like your sweater to look like? Draw a picture of it on Page 75.

My sweater ...

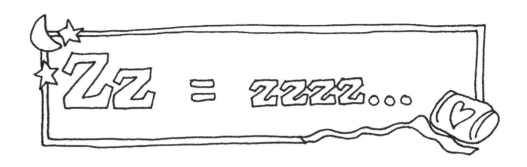

Pronounced: zeez

The Christmas season is long in Sweden – from the first part of December (Advent Sunday) to Knutdagen (January 13). Although there are busy times, there are also many relaxing times. And there are times for naps and for sleeping ... zzzz! Relax! Sleep well!

- Pronounce the Swedish word. Color the heading and picture above.
- How do you like to relax? When and where do you take a nap? What is your bedtime? Do you have a cat or dog or other animal that sleeps beside you?

Pronounced: oak-tuur

Christmas. Snow. Beautiful lights in the city and countryside. Bundled up for the cold. It's **time** "to go for a ride" (åktur). How about going for a ride on a sled? There's a special sled in Sweden called a kicksled. It's lots of fun!

- Pronounce the Swedish word. Color the heading and the picture above.
- On Page 81, draw a picture of what you would go in or on for a Christmas ride. Is it a car? A snowmobile? A canoe or boat? A sled? A kicksled? Something else?

79

My Christmas ride ...

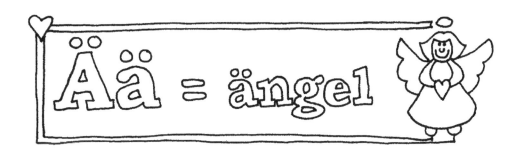

Pronounced: engell (g as in the word good)

Ängel (angel) ornaments are a Swedish tradition. Although they can be made out of paper or yarn or wood, many are made of straw. Hearts and stars are also popular straw ornaments. The julbock (yule buck), a Christmas goat, is also made of straw. It is decorated with red cloth ribbon and often sits at the base of the Christmas tree. Years ago, a goat would lead the sleigh bringing the gifts.

- Pronounce the Swedish word. Color the heading and the picture above.
- What are your favorite Christmas ornaments? What are they made of?
- What would you like to place on the floor near your Christmas tree this year? A julbock? A manger? A special toy? Something else?

Pronounced: unsk-e-lista

This is the last of the 29 letters in the Swedish alphabet. We have explored many Swedish traditions, and this is our final one for this Christmas season. Önskelista is a wish list. Children will make a list of what they would like Santa to bring them on Christmas Eve.

- Pronounce the Swedish word. Color the heading and picture above.
- What is or was on your wish list for Christmas?
- Here's another kind of wish: What do you wish for during the next year? For yourself? For your family? For your friends? For your neighborhood, your country and our world? Write them out on Page 87, our book's final page.

85

My wish list ...

tomte/jultomte hunt answer: 17

Pages 1, 3, 6, 18, 25, 30, 2 on 33, 35, 41, 46, 3 on 51, 61, 71, 77

14897418R00051